Selected Poems of Jules Breton
From the Letters of Vincent van Gogh

Jules Breton

Translated from the French with Commentary by

Sharon Fish Mooney

RESOURCE *Publications* • Eugene, Oregon

SELECTED POEMS OF JULES BRETON
From the Letters of Vincent van Gogh

Copyright © 2024 Sharon Fish Mooney. All rights reserved. Except for brief quotations in critical publications or reviews, no part of this book may be reproduced in any manner without prior written permission from the publisher. Write: Permissions, Wipf and Stock Publishers, 199 W. 8th Ave., Suite 3, Eugene, OR 97401.

Resource Publications
An Imprint of Wipf and Stock Publishers
199 W. 8th Ave., Suite 3
Eugene, OR 97401

www.wipfandstock.com

PAPERBACK ISBN: 979-8-3852-1540-9
HARDCOVER ISBN: 979-8-3852-1541-6
EBOOK ISBN: 979-8-3852-1542-3

Quotations from Vincent van Gogh's letters appear by permission from Vincent van Gogh – The Letters. Leo Jansen, Hans Luijten, and Nienke Bakker (eds.). Van Gogh Museum & Huygens Institute, Amsterdam 2009: Version: October 2021: https://vangoghletters.org/
© Van Gogh Museum.

"Sharon Mooney, whose book of ekphrastic poems inspired by Van Gogh's paintings established her as a master of the sonnet, now shows that she is a literary translator of the highest order. Jules Breton's poems, though fluent in diction, are tight and dense in imagery, rendering them particularly difficult to translate into English, let alone English that echoes the rhymes of the originals. Mooney's renditions have the musical flow that characterizes the French poems and brings them fully into life in English. This is a small masterpiece of literary translation."
—Jonathan Chaves, translator and professor of Chinese, The George Washington University

"Jules Breton was as gifted with the pen as he was with the brush. We have seen the beauty of his paintings, and now, thanks to Sharon Fish Mooney's masterful translations, we can also see the beauty of his poetry. The translator's gifts have gifted us with the gifts of this great and under-appreciated poet. May her work make his work as well known and well-loved as it deserves to be."
—Joseph Pearce, editor, *St. Austin Review*

"Sharon Mooney's idea of translating the poems found in Van Gogh's letters was an inspiration. They're all very good poems, some of them breathtakingly beautiful. Though Mooney took great care in fashioning her English versions, they read as though they'd been written effortlessly, appearing on the page fully realized. Her commentary shows Breton at the center of a vibrant creative circle, generous in his admiration of his peers, and worthy of their admiration and ours."
—Alfred Nicol, poet and translator of *One Hundred Visions of War*

"Selected Poems of Jules Breton is a valuable introduction to the work of a French painter-poet adored by Vincent van Gogh and yet virtually unknown to English readers. Sharon Mooney's masterful metrical translations and insightful commentary on this 'poet with the pen as well as with the brush' offer us an intriguing window into the intimate relationship between painting and poetry."
—Katherine M. Hedeen, professor of Spanish and literary translation, Kenyon College

"This small volume is a treasure trove of verse and imagery. Sharon Mooney's adept translations of Breton's poems are a pleasure to read, and her commentaries are insightful. From the still-life of *Autumn* to the 'Shadows . . . tinged / All around with a golden thread' in *Twilight*, these poems invite us to savor Breton's meditative perspective on rural life, and they also deepen our understanding of Van Gogh both as a person and as an artist."
—Molly Lynde-Recchia, professor of French, Western Michigan University

Selected Poems of Jules Breton
From the Letters of Vincent van Gogh

Jules Breton, 1890
Artist and Poet

Contents

Introduction / 9
    Jules Breton the Artist
    Jules Breton the Poet
    Jules Breton and Vincent van Gogh
    Translation Issues and Commentary
    Conclusion

Selected Poems with Commentary / 15
    Les cigales (À Leconte de Lisle) / *Cicadas* (To Leconte de Lisle) / 17
    Automne (À Jules Dupré) / *Autumn* (To Jules Dupré) / 21
    Soleil couchant (À mon frère Émile Breton)
            Sunset (To my brother Émile Breton) / 25
    Yvonne (À André Lemoyne)/ *Yvonne* (To André Lemoyne) / 29
    L'aube (À Corot) / *Dawn* (To Corot) / 32
    Le soir (À Louis Cabat) / *Evening* (To Louis Cabat) / 36
    Seule (À Georges Lafenestre) / *Alone* (To Georges Lafenestre) / 39
    Le retour des champs (À François Millet) /
            Return from the Fields (To François Millet) / 43
    Illusions (À Anatole France) / *Illusions* (To Anatole France) / 48
    Dans la plaine / *On the Plain* / 51
    Crépuscule (À Charles Daubigny) / *Twilight* (To Charles Daubigny) / 55
    Le chant du soir / *Song of the Evening* / 61
    Les ruines / *The Ruins* / 67
    Les deux croix (À Robert-Fleury) / *Two Crosses* (To Robert-Fleury) / 70

Book References and Select Bibliography / 74
Translator's Poem Credits / 77
Acknowledgments / 78
About the Translator / 80

The art of the poet is more intoxicating than that of the painter; for the succession of the tableaux and the thoughts, the rapidity of the images, the intensity of the sentiments, and the immateriality of the process, tend to maintain in the brain and the nervous system a perpetual and pleasing excitement. Painting, on the contrary, employs itself in the interpretation of a simple idea by palpable means. But how many resemblances there are between the two arts! In both there are the same general laws of composition, of comparison, of rejection, of contrast, and of harmony.

    Jules Breton in *The Life of an Artist: An Autobiography*
    Mary J. Serrano (Translator), pp. 333–334

INTRODUCTION

Jules Breton the Artist

Jules Adolphe Aimé Louis Breton was born May 1, 1827 in Courrières, Artois, France. He died in Paris on July 5, 1906. Breton was a Realist artist of peasant and religious themes and well-known for his oil paintings of French rural life. His art was very popular in Europe in the late nineteenth century. His mother died when he was four years old and he was brought up by his father, a well-to-do landowner and manager of the estate of the Duke of Duras.

At age sixteen Breton met the well-known Belgian artist Félix De Vigne who was influential in Breton's development as an artist. In 1843 Breton left his family home to study at the Royal Academy of Fine Arts in Ghent, Belgium under the tutelage of De Vigne and Belgian artist Henri Van der Haert. From Ghent he moved to Antwerp, continuing with his art studies and copying the paintings of master artists. In 1847 he moved back to France to study at the École des Beaux-Arts in Paris. Breton's initial paintings were historical in nature and heavily influenced by the French Revolution of 1848; his *Misère et Désespoir/ Misery and Despair* and *Faim/ Hunger* were displayed at the Salon de Paris.

In France, in the 1850's, Breton returned to his first love: the French countryside. He also married Élodie De Vigne, the daughter of Félix De Vigne. Breton exhibited his work at the Salon de Paris and received several awards. At the 1867 Universal Exposition in Paris he received a first-class medal for his art. He was elected to the Académie des Beaux-Arts in 1886. Raised as a Catholic, many of his poems reflect his upbringing and various Church traditions; his faith influenced both his art and poetry. He painted and wrote poetry related to Christian religious festivals and rites in Brittany, like the penitential pardons, in addition to paintings and poems depicting rural peasant life in France and his love of nature.

Breton became well known in America for his 1884 oil on canvas, *Le chant de l'alouette/The Song of the Lark* (Henry Field Memorial Collection, Art Institute of Chicago). It was exhibited at the Chicago World's Fair in 1934 where First Lady Eleanor Roosevelt stated it was her own favorite painting and it won the *Chicago Daily News* contest to find the most beloved work of art in America. Willa Cather's 1915 novel, *The Song of the Lark*, takes its name from this painting. In 2014 the actor Bill Murray made the claim when he was being interviewed for his role in the movie *The Monuments Men* that this was the painting that may have saved his life when he was contemplating suicide. (See Book References and Select Bibliography for various resources consulted on Breton's history and an on-line interview with Bill Murray).

Jules Breton the Poet

Breton is less well-known in America, if known at all, for his poetry, but his poetry, as well as his art, served to define his life. His poems, rooted in the metrical literary traditions of the Victorian era in which he lived, were published during his lifetime in a number of journals and in books: *Jeanne/Jeanne*, a novel in verse, *Les Champs et la mer/The Fields and the Sea*, a collection of poems, and *Œuvres Poétiques de Jules Breton /Poetic Works of Jules Breton, 1867–1887*.

In a letter to Breton in 1875 poet and literary critic Eugène Manuel wrote:

> Today I have no hesitation in telling you that you are a poet with the pen as well as with the brush, and an excellent poet. The same deep sense of nature which has inspired so many wonderful paintings, you have found it and managed to reproduce it equally purely, seriously and penetratingly with words, sound, rhythms and images (cited in Lacouture, p. 185).

Other poets and art critics also expressed admiration and delight in Breton's dual artistic roles.

Jules Breton and Vincent van Gogh

My interest in Breton was sparked while doing research in the Van Gogh Museum Library, Amsterdam, The Netherlands for my own book of ekphrastic poetry: *Bending Toward Heaven: Poems After the Art of Vincent van Gogh*. Van Gogh (1853–1890) made reference to Breton's art and poetry numerous times in letters to friends and family members and considered Breton one of his most admired artists and poets.

In 1884, Van Gogh sent twelve of Breton's poems he had copied from Breton's book of French poetry in a letter to Anthon van Rappard (1858–1892), an artist friend and mentor. (Van Gogh Letter 435 to Van Rappard) Nine years earlier he had sent a poem by Breton to his younger brother, Theo (1857–1891), with the promise of sending him Breton's complete book of poetry, *Les Champs et la mer*. Van Gogh also included one of Breton's poems that had been previously published in a journal in a poetry album he sent to his brother. They both loved Breton's art. Theo was a Dutch art dealer.

In 1880 Van Gogh walked 85 kilometers roundtrip to Courrières hoping to find work to help support himself. He also saw, while there, the outside of Breton's studio, noting it was "...newly built in brick, of a Methodist regularity." He wrote to his brother, Theo, that he didn't dare to introduce himself so never did meet Breton personally. (Van Gogh Letter 158 to Theo)

Translation Issues and Commentary

The poems I have included in this book are the poems by Breton that Van Gogh included in his correspondence to Theo and to Anthon van Rappard. The poems sent to Van Rappard have been published and translated very faithfully into English in *Vincent van*

Gogh: The Letters, but without strict adherence to rhyme or meter. My desire was to maintain metrical structures comparable to the original poems. This has necessitated, at times, substitutions or equivalents, though I hoped to adhere to both language and imagery that mirrored the spirit of the metrical literary traditions of the Romantic and Victorian eras in which Breton lived and wrote and the character and personality of Breton himself. (For translations of the poems sent to Van Rappard published in the Van Gogh Museum Letters see: https://vangoghletters.org/vg/letters/let435/letter.html)

Exact and sometimes even approximate equivalents I believe are not always possible in translated poetry, and even less so with metrical poetry translations. My hope is that I have captured both the meaning and the spirit of each poem.

One of the most helpful pieces of advice I received when beginning my venture into French translation was "get to know your poet." I have tried to do that as much as possible by reading Breton's autobiography, *La Vie d'un artiste/The Life of an Artist: An Autobiography* (1890), translated into English by Mary J. Serrano (1840–1923). Reading and rereading Van Gogh's letters and all his references to Breton has also helped me appreciate his art and poetry.

In my commentaries that accompany each poem, I have chosen to speculate on why the poem might have been written. Over half of the poems in Breton's complete book of poetry are dedicated to well known artists and poets. I found myself wondering as I read them if some of the poems may have been written to reflect in some way the poet or artist the poem was dedicated to. I also speculate on that in my commentary as well as why Van Gogh might have chosen it to send to his brother or Dutch artist Anthon van Rappard.

Conclusion

In an interview with William Baer for his book, *Thirteen on Form: Conversations with Poets*, poet and translator Rhina P. Espaillat stated: "The primary job of the translator is to carry the poem from one language to the other with as little damage as possible." (Baer, p. 295) My hope is that I have been able to accomplish that goal.

SELECTED POEMS WITH COMMENTARY

Les cigales (À Leconte de Lisle)

Lorsque dans l'herbe mûre aucun épi ne bouge,
Qu'à l'ardeur des rayons crépite le froment,
Que le coquelicot tombe languissamment
Sous le faible fardeau de sa corolle rouge;

Tous les oiseaux de l'air ont fait taire leurs chants;
Les ramiers paresseux, au plus noir des ramures,
Somnolents, dans les bois, ont cessé leurs murmures,
Loin du soleil muet incendiant les champs.

Dans les blés, cependant, d'intrépides cigales,
Jetant leurs mille bruits, fanfare de l'été,
Ont frénétiquement et sans trêve agité
Leurs ailes sur l'airain de leurs folles cymbales.

Frémissantes, debout sur les longs épis d'or,
Virtuoses qui vont s'éteindre avant l'automne,
Elles poussaient au ciel leur hymne monotone
Qui dans l'ombre des nuits retentissait encor.

Et rien n'arrêtera leurs cris intarissables;
Quand on les chassera de l'avoine et des blés,
Elles émigreront sur les buissons brûlés
Qui se meurent de soif dans les déserts de sables.

Sur l'arbuste effeuillé, sur les chardons flétris
Qui laissent s'envoler leur blanche chevelure,
On reverra l'insecte à la forte encolure,
Plein d'ivresse, toujours s'exalter dans ses cris;

Jusqu'à ce qu'ouvrant l'aile en lambeaux arrachée,
Exaspéré, brûlant d'un feu toujours plus pur,
Son œil de bronze fixe et tendu vers l'azur,
Il expire en chantant sur la tige séchée.

Courrières, 1873

Cicadas (To Leconte de Lisle)

When in ripe summer fields the sun beats down
Crackling wheat and stilling the ears of corn,
Under the burden of its round red crown
The poppy languishes, tired and worn.

All birds have ceased to sing; their song is done.
The lazy pigeons on the blackest boughs
Drowse in the woods, no murmurings now
Far from the fields burned by the silent sun.

Yet in the corn intrepid cicadas beat
Their wings, a thousand strong, buckling tymbals.
With frantic energy, summer's fanfare sweet,
They sound like they are playing on brass cymbals.

Quivering on long golden ears of grain
The virtuosos stand who soon will die,
Before autumn comes, intoning to a sky
That in night shadows echoes their hymn's refrain.

Nothing will stop their inexhaustible cries.
When from oats and wheat, small cicadas are chased
They migrate into burnt bushes soon to die
Of thirst beneath scorched and desert-like wastes.

You'll see one on a shriveled, leafless shrub,
Strong-necked insect on thistles whose white hair flies
Or on a discolored and withered prickly stub,
Filled with rapture, exalting in final cries

Until it opens its tattered wings to lie
Exhausted, burning, chanting its requiem.
With bronze eyes fixed and straining toward the sky
It expires, singing, on the dried-up stem.

Courrières, 1873

Les cigales/Cicadas

Les cigales was written in *Courrières* in 1873. Breton would have been very familiar with the summer sounds of the cicadas, or *cigales* as they are called in France. They are very active in Provence and other regions of southern France from May to October. Male cicadas make their harsh cries heard to attract female cicadas by expanding and contracting a membrane in the abdomen called a tymbal. Breton may not have known that they did this but he was certainly familiar with the harsh sound they made and, according to his poem, he was well aware that it sounded like the clashing of cymbals (*cymbales*).

Leconte de Lisle (1818–1894) was a French non-fiction writer and translator of Greek tragedies. He was also a poet and leader of the Parnassian poetic movement (1866). In contrast to the Romantic movement, these poets stressed emotional detachment in their poetry. Like Breton, Leconte de Lisle was also witness to the French Revolution. The *Encyclopedia Britannica* notes that from 1865 to 1895 he was acknowledged as the foremost French poet apart from Victor Hugo.

In his autobiography Breton wrote the following:

> Passing through Paris, I had bought at the railway-station Lemerre's *Anthologie*. I must confess, to my shame, that for the first time I read there some verses of Leconte de Lisle. They had enchanted me...with their magnificent rhythm, their splendor of diction, the tragic horrors of their images, their profound insight into the spiritual, their wonderful melody, resounded ceaselessly in my memory and held me captive by their spell. (*Autobiography*, p. 327)

Living in France, Leconte de Lisle, like Breton, would have been well acquainted with cicadas. Breton also regularly visited the coastal region of Brittany in the west of France and painted there. De Lisle lived in Brittany for many years.

Les Cigales would have appealed to Van Gogh for a variety of reasons. In a letter to Theo sent from Arles in July, 1888, Vincent wrote about just returning from a visit to Fontvieille, a village in Provence, and noted the cicadas there "...sing at least as loudly as a frog." (Letter 638)

In a letter to both Theo and Theo's wife Johanna, July 6, 1889 from Saint-Rémy-de-Provence, Van Gogh waxes eloquently on the cicadas.

> I think I'm lucky to be able to read or re-read this (Shakespeare's *Henry VIII*) at my leisure, and then I very much hope to read Homer at last. Outside the cicadas are singing fit to burst, a strident cry ten times louder than that of the crickets, and the scorched grass is taking on beautiful tones of old gold. And the beautiful towns of the south are in the state of our dead towns along the Zuiderzee, which were formerly lively. While in the downfall and the decline of things, the cicadas dear to good old Socrates have remained. And here, certainly, they're still singing old Greek. (Letter 787)

In Plato's *Phaedrus*, Socrates and his student Phaedrus are sitting on a riverbank amid a chorus of cicadas. In Greek mythology, cicadas were once humans. Enchanted by the Muses they died, but were rewarded with the gift of singing from birth to death.

Vincent wrote to Theo again on July 14th or 15th from Saint-Rémy-de-Provence and said: "I enclose a croquis (sketch) of the cicadas from here. Their song in times of great heat holds the same charm for me as the cricket in the peasant's hearth at home." (Letter 790) In September he wrote again, promising to send Theo some of his paintings that included one of olive trees and wrote that "...I've tried to express the time of day when one sees the green beetles and the cicadas flying in the heat." (Letter 805)

Automne (À Jules Dupré)

La rivière s'écoule avec lenteur. Ses eaux
Murmurent, près du bord, aux souches des vieux aulnes
Qui se teignent de sang; de hauts peupliers jaunes
Sèment leurs feuilles d'or parmi les blonds roseaux.

Le vent léger, qui croise en mobiles réseaux
Ses rides d'argent clair, laisse de sombres zones
Où les arbres plongeant leurs dômes et leurs cônes
Tremblent, comme agités par des milliers d'oiseaux.

Par instants se répète un cri grêle de grive,
Et, lancé brusquement des herbes de la rive,
Étincelle un joyau dans l'air subtil et bleu;

Un chant aigu prolonge une note stridente;
C'est le martin-pêcheur qui fuit d'une aile ardente
Dans un furtif rayon d'émeraude et de feu.

Courrières, 1875

Autumn (To Jules Dupré)

The river slowly flows; its waters weave
Their way round stumps of alders, stained blood-red.
Tall yellow poplars scatter their golden leaves
Among blond flaxen reeds. The riverbed

Awakes and murmurs as a soft wind moans
And blows clear silver wrinkles from dark regions,
Where trembling trees dip down their domes and cones
As if agitated by birds in the thousands.

A thrush repeats its sharp and tiny cry.
Then, darting from the grassy shore it sings
And sparkles, jewel-like in the clear blue sky

As its prolonged note is heard, pitched shrill and higher—
The kingfisher takes flight on flaming wings
In a furtive ray of emerald and of fire.

Courrières, 1875

Automne/Autumn

Automne was written in 1875. Though titled for a season of the year, its most prominent feature is a kingfisher taking flight from the riverbank on flaming wings. In his autobiography Breton tells about his childhood and walking with his grand-mother. He writes about the sweet songs of the larks, golden blossoms, butterflies, and the kingfisher:

> But as we crossed the wooden bridge over the little river, oh! first surprise! A wonderful bird darts from the bank, uttering a shrill and prolonged cry. Its breast is of fire, and its back of a splendid green... "A kingfisher," my grandmother tells me. (*Autobiography*, pp. 39–40)

Automne is dedicated to French artist Jules Dupré (1811–1889). Dupré was a primary member of the Barbazon school of landscape painters. He first exhibited at the Salon in 1831 and was awarded a second-class medal in 1834. Breton, who also exhibited at the Salon, would have been very familiar with Dupré's art. Breton's choice of subject for his poem would have appealed to Dupré's love of nature. An 1850 oil on canvas by Dupré is titled *Autumn Landscape*.

Van Gogh sent this poem to his artist friend Van Rappard on March 8, 1884. On March 13th he sent this same friend a drawing of a kingfisher he had done. (Letters 435 & 437) Earlier he had sent him a sketch of his family's parsonage garden in winter and noted it had sent him dreaming, perhaps, in part, about kingfishers.

On March 20th of the same year he wrote the following to Theo from Nuenen:

> For this month I have some pen drawings for you; in the first place the ones that are with Rappard at the moment—about which I have a letter from him that he thought they were ALL beautiful, and the sentiment in Behind the hedgerows and the Kingfisher PARTICULARLY beautiful. (Letter 440)

Van Gogh's oil on canvas, *Kingfisher by the Waterside*, was painted in 1887. Was this painting perhaps inspired, in part, by Breton's poem? Gerard Manley Hopkins, the painter who became a priest and poet and who, like Van Gogh, was a frequenter of art museums in Europe and France, wrote his well-known poem, *As Kingfishers Catch Fire* in 1877. Was he, too, perhaps influenced to some degree by Breton's art and poetry?

Soleil couchant (À mon frère Émile Breton)

Des vapeurs aux remous infinis, mer de brume
Où les coteaux voilés ondulent, larges flots,
Les villages, perdus comme de noirs îlots,
Émergent, enfonçant leurs pieds bruns dans l'écume.

Tandis que tout se tait, s'agrandit, nage et fume,
Qu'au fond des ravins, seuls, tintent de lents grelots,
Que de rares lueurs, ainsi que des falots,
Palpitent; le ciel vibre et tout entier s'allume.

Notre globe muet, sous le dôme vermeil,
Prie et rêve ébloui par la magnificence
De l'astre fécondant que le nuage encense;

Et dans ce grand respect, pris d'un divin sommeil,
Orbe rouge au milieu de l'auréole immense,
Gravement, lentement se couche le soleil.

Douarnenez, 1873

Sunset (To my brother Émile Breton)

Unending mist and swirling vapors meet,
shrouding the hills in undulating waves.
Villages, like lost islands once enslaved,
emerge, sink in the foam their dusky feet.

While all is hushed, mist rises to complete
the day; cowbells ring slow in low ravines
and lights like lanterns flicker, start to gleam
in a sky that vibrates, glows with light replete.

Our silent globe, vermillion canopied
now prays and dreams, awed by magnificence;
the fertile star burns through the clouds like incense.

With honor and divine sleep overcome,
haloed like a saint, crowned round like royalty,
solemnly, slowly sets the red-orbed sun.

    Douarnenez, 1873

Soleil couchant / Song of the Evening

It is not surprising that Breton would have dedicated this poem to Émile, one of his younger brothers. Émile Adélard Breton (1831–1902) was also an artist and an engraver whose paintings included nocturnal scenes and sunsets. One of his oil on canvas paintings is titled *Coucher de soleil à l'orée de la forêt (Sunset on the Edge of the Forest)*. Another is *Un coucher de soleil d'hiver (A Winter Sunset)*. Evening is a subject of a number of Breton's poems.

In January 1874 Vincent wrote to Theo from London and included a list of painters "whom I like very much indeed." Both Jules and Émile Breton were on the list. (Letter 017) When Van Gogh was in Paris in 1875 working for Goupil and Co. he visited the Musée du Luxembourg in Paris with another worker who was living with him at the time and showed him the paintings he liked best there. One was *Winter Evening* by Émile Breton; three others were by Jules Breton. (Letter 055) From May 1875 to April 1976 Van Gogh worked in Paris. He had begun as an apprentice at The Hague branch of Goupil and Co. at age sixteen. Goupil and Co. was an art dealership specializing in prints and engravings with reproductions of works by European Salon artists. Theo also worked for this same company as an art dealer. Goupil had branches in several European countries including the Netherlands, France and London. Vincent worked in all three.

Vincent wrote to Theo about one of Émile's paintings titled *Sunday Morning in Winter* that was currently in a Goupil gallery where he was working. This painting, like the poem *Illusions* by Jules Breton that he also sent in the same letter, would have reminded both brothers of their family upbringing. Their father was a Protestant minister in the Netherlands and the boys grew up attending his church. About the painting Vincent wrote:

You know it, don't you? It's a village street with farmhouses and sheds, and at the end the church surrounded by poplars. Everything covered with snow and little black figures going to church. It tells us that winter is cold but that there are warm human hearts. (Letter 061)

Vincent created a number of paintings of churches, including one in 1884 for his parents of the congregation leaving his father's Reformed church in Nuenen. Like the parishioners in Breton's painting, they were also depicted as little black figures.

Yvonne (À André Lemoyne)

Je regardais souvent, le coude à la fenêtre,
Les filles revenir de la source à midi.
Yvonne apparaissait, et son geste hardi,
Son haut galbe de loin la faisait reconnaître.

C'était pour le regard une fête, parbleu!
Que de la suivre alors, si droite sous sa cruche,
Quand, relevant sa coiffe en huppe de perruche,
Le vent faisait flotter son souple jupon bleu.

Avec quelle beauté, laissant son humble châle
Tomber en nobles plis que la brise inclinait,
Elle étendait le bras, en l'air, et retenait
Son amphore de grès rouge sur son front pâle!

Que ses traits étaient purs! Je ne sais quoi d'amer
Et de charmant errait sur sa lèvre sauvage;
Et comme elle était bien la fille du rivage,
Forte et comme trempée aux souffles de la mer!

Par la rue aux rumeurs banales et narquoises,
Où quelques maigres chiens, craintifs, se font la cour,
Parmi de vils ramas poussés de mainte cour
Au ruisseaux où le ciel reflète ses turquoises,

De la ville rasant les murs gris ou crayeux,
Je crois la voir encor, une main sur la hanche,
Sans que de l'urne pleine une goutte s'épanche,
Grande et grave passer sans détourner les yeux.

Saint-Pol de Léon, 1873

Yvonne (To André Lemoyne)

Leaning on the sill I often watched
The girls at noon returning from the spring.
Yet one appeared, so stately, proud and tall.
Her name? Yvonne. She made my heart to sing.

Feast for sore eyes she was, indeed.
A pitcher on her head, she walked upright,
Wind blowing her blue petticoat and with
Her hair upswept, reflecting the sun's light,

Beauty enhanced by folds of a humble shawl
That fell with summer's breeze in noble folds,
Red clay amphora resting on pale brow,
Her arm stretched up to balance and to hold.

How pure her features, yet upon her lip
There played a wandering look, savage and free.
She truly was the daughter of the shore,
Charming yet strong as tides are in the sea.

Now in the street of rumors, taunts and cries
Where skinny fearful dogs are now a courting,
Amidst vile refuse swept from many a yard
In turquoise streams, from the blue sky reflecting,

Now from this city, walls chalky and grey
I think I see her, hand on hip, today.
Urn on her head, just brimming yet not spilling,
Grand, grave she passes, doesn't look away.

Saint-Pol de Léon, 1873

Yvonne/Yvonne

Breton was noted for his many paintings of peasant women in the fields, both in groups and singly. It is not surprising one of his poems would also feature one of the peasant women he painted. Critics have often noted his paintings of peasants presented a rather romanticized view compared to the more rustic realism of Jean-François Millet.

A number of his paintings feature individual peasant women coming home from the fields with one arm upheld to hold securely something on their head. That something might be a basket of fruit, a sack of potatoes, a sheaf of wheat or a clay jug for water or wine.

French poet André Lemoyne (1822–1907), to whom this poem is dedicated, was also a writer of novels. He was librarian of the School of Decorative Arts in Paris.

Vincent van Gogh, The Letters, includes what at first glance seems to be a letter addressed to Jules Breton from Van Gogh but it is unclear, the editors note, if this actually was. He does include one stanza of this poem at the end of the letter. (Letter RM05) There are no other mentions of this poem in his letters other than the one he sent to Van Rappard. It would probably have appealed to Van Gogh as he often used peasant women as his models.

Van Gogh sent a copy of Lemoyne's poem *Soirèe d'hiver (A Winter Evening)* to his brother. (Letter RM02 & Pabst, p. 87) The poem is very similar in style and content to those of Breton's with a focus both on the beauties of nature (clumps of red oaks, little junipers, holly bushes, woodpeckers) and a rural father carrying beech wood for a fire home on his shoulder to brighten the corners of his house and delight his children.

L'aube (À Corot)

Je suivais un sentier, à l'aube, dans les blés,
Étroit, où l'on se mouille aux gouttes qui s'épanchent
En frôlant les épis alourdis qui se penchent;
Et j'errais évoquant mes rêves envolés.

Ah! qui n'a pas perdu des rameaux étoilés,
Comme les saules gris que les hommes ébranchent,
Qui font un bruit si doux quand leurs larmes étanchent
La soif des liserons à leurs pieds enroulés!

Et je sentais mon cœur, d'où je chassais la prose,
S'attendrir au rayon discret, pâle et changeant
Comme un arbre souffrant et que la pluie arrose.

Et voilà que, joyeuse, éclate au ciel d'argent
L'alouette qui voit, des brumes émergeant,
A l'Orient monter le premier flocon rose.

Courrières, 1872

Dawn (To Corot)

I followed a path, at dawn, a narrow way
Into the wheat, brushed against bending ears
Heavy with dew; they drenched me with their tears.
I wandered, called forth dreams long flown away.

Ah! Dawn brings loss of sparkling branches sweet,
Like the gray willows men cut back, that break,
Making a soft sound as their teardrops slake
The thirst of bindweed curled around their feet.

I felt my heart where prose once seemed so strong
Grow soft in changing light, felt gently kissed,
Much like an injured tree, watered by rain.

Now joy bursts from the silver heavens again.
The lark now sees emerging from the mist
In the east the first pink fleck of dawn.

    Courrières, 1872

L'aube/Dawn

Breton was a lover of larks, judging from both his art and his poetry. One of his most popular paintings, *The Song of the Lark*, features a lark emerging in song from the mist in the dawn. In his autobiography he writes of his childhood memories when he "...was awakened by the song of the birds in the morning when the sunrise lighted up the room with a rosy flame that grew paler and paler in the light of an opal sky...". (*Autobiography*, p. 227)

Breton dedicated *L'aube* to Jean-Baptiste-Camille Corot (1796–1875) who was a French artist well-known for his landscapes and portraits. Corot also painted the dawn in an oil on panel (c.1865–70) with the same title as Breton's 1872 poem. Corot spent much of his life in the French countryside and his plein-air style appealed to many other painters of the era, including Breton, whose paintings and poems, like *L'aube*, focused on the nature that surrounded him.

Corot was one of Breton's favorite artists. After viewing an art Exhibition he wrote about Corot's art in his autobiography, of "...the incomparable Corots, so resplendent with ideal beauty that they transport one to heaven, so true to Nature that in seeing them one fancies one is looking through an open window upon Nature's self!" (*Autobiography*, p. 347)

Breton also wrote that Corot did him "the distinguished honor" of visiting him in Courrières in 1860 and noted: "We walked through the woods and the plains, indulging all the way in expressions of childlike delight. The merest nothing, a bud freshly opened, the tender shoot of a plant, was sufficient to launch him into poetry, and what poetry!" (*Autobiography*, pp. 348–349)

His final tribute to Corot reads: "Each of his landscapes is a hymn of serene purity, where everything, however, lives, rejoices, loves, and palpitates." (*Autobiography*, p. 350)

Van Gogh was also a lover of larks and, too, of Breton's painting. In May, 1885, Vincent wrote to Theo from Nuenen: "How fine, though, I think Jules Breton's *The song of the lark...*" (Letter 500) In a letter sent home to his father and mother in the Netherlands in April, 1876 he notes that on the train, before arriving at the London station, "Even before the sun rose I heard a lark." (Letter 076) He makes frequent mentions of larks in other letters to Theo.

Corot was also one of Van Gogh's favorite artists. In a letter to Theo dated May 31, 1875, Van Gogh references both Breton and Corot, noting he saw Breton, probably at Goupil and Co. He also wrote that he visited the Corot retrospective exhibition held in the École Nationale des Beaux-Arts shortly after Corot's death and especially appreciated his painting *Christ on The Mount of Olives*. (Letter 034) This painting would have appealed to him from a religious perspective and might also have been inspiration for some of his own future oil paintings of olive trees and olive groves.

Le soir – (À Louis Cabat)

C'est un humble fossé perdu sous le feuillage;
Les aunes du bosquet le couvrent à demi;
L'insecte, en l'effleurant, trace un léger sillage
Et s'en vient seul rayer le miroir endormi.

Le soir tombe, et c'est l'heure où se fait le miracle,
Transfiguration qui change tout en or;
Aux yeux charmés tout offre un ravissant spectacle;
Le modeste fossé brille plus qu'un trésor.

Le ciel éblouissant, tamisé par les branches,
A plongé dans l'eau noire un lumineux rayon;
Tombant de tous côtés, des étincelles blanches
Entourent un foyer d'or pâle en fusion.

Aux bords tout est mystère et douceur infinie.
On y voit s'assoupir quelques fleurs aux tons froids,
Et les reflets confus de verdure brunie
Et d'arbres violets qui descendent tout droits.

Dans la lumière, au loin, des touffes d'émeraude
Vous laissent deviner la ligne des champs blonds,
Et le ciel enflammé d'une teinte si chaude,
Et le soleil tombé qui tremble dans les joncs.

Et dans mon âme émue, alors quand je compare
L'humilité du site à sa sublimité,
un délire sacré de mon esprit s'empare,
Et j'entrevois la main de la divinité.

Ce n'est rien et c'est tout. En créant la nature
Dieu répandit partout la splendeur de l'effet;
Aux petits des oiseaux s'il donne la pâture,
Il prodigue le beau, ce suprême bienfait.

Ce n'est rien et c'est tout. En le voyant j'oublie,
Pauvre petit fossé qui me troubles si fort,
Mes angoisses de cœur, mes rêves d'Italie,
Et je me sens meilleur, et je bénis le sort.

Courrières, 1867

Evening (To Louis Cabat)

A humble ditch is lost beneath foliage,
Half covered by a grove of alder trees.
Etched on its channel there's a trace, a trail
An insect on its winding surface leaves.

The evening falls, it's time for the miracle
When all is transformed to gold, without measure.
A vision entrancing to delighted eyes,
The humble ditch shines brighter than a treasure.

The dazzling sky now filters through the branches.
In black water it plunges deep its ray,
While all around white sparks seem to be falling
Upon earth's golden hearth at close of day.

While on the ditch's banks there is sweet mystery;
Pale flowers go to sleep with nodding heads,
Blurred reflections of brown, burnished greenery,
Of purple shadows, trees going to bed.

In the far distance are flaxen-colored fields
Surrounded by emerald clusters from the sun
That's setting. Now it flickers in the rushes.
Ablaze with fiery hues, the day is done.

My spirit stirs, is moved when I compare
This unpretentious site to the sublime.
An ecstasy most sacred captures my soul.
I catch a glimpse of the hand of the Divine.

It is but a trifle, yet it is everything.
In nature God spreads glory all about.
He gives the birds' poor tiny chicks their food.
Blessings supreme He lavishly pours out.

It is but a trifle, yet it is everything,
Poor little ditch. What troubles me of late?
I look on you, forget my anxieties,
My dreams of Italy, and bless my fate.

Courrières, 1867

Le soir/Evening

In his autobiography Breton writes that he composed his first sonnet, *Courrières*, in 1864 and notes: "Shortly afterward, inspired by the view of a pool sleeping in the shadow of the alders, I composed a little poem called *Le Soir*, which, like the sonnet just mentioned, is included in the collection, *Les Champs et la mer*." (*Autobiography*, p. 329)

Breton made his first trip to Italy in 1863; some of his paintings may have been painted in Italy or inspired by his travels there. One example is his 1863 painting titled *Water Carriers*. Two girls in the painting are collecting water from a spring near what is probably the Mediterranean Sea. (See: https://www.stairsainty.com/artwork/water-carriers/) He made a second trip to Italy in 1870 and, while there, viewed the Sistine chapel and Giotto's frescoes.

Louis-Nicolas Cabat (1812–1893) was a French landscape painter and member of the Académie des Beaux-Arts of the Institut de France. This poem could have appealed to him due to its reference to Italy. Cabat was also a member of the Accademia di San Luca, an academy of artists in Rome, and was director of the French Academy in Rome from 1879 to 1884. His landscapes, like Breton's, were usually based on the French countryside.

This poem may have appealed to Van Gogh for several reasons. Cabat's *The Pond at Ville-d'Avray* and *Autumnal Evening* were among his favorites paintings that he showed to his friend in the Luxembourg museum. (Letter 055) In January, 1876, Vincent wrote Theo enclosing a lithograph for him by Cabat. He wrote: "Cabat is a lot like Ruisdael, there are two magnificent paintings by him in the Luxembourg, one a pond with trees around it in the autumn at sunset, and the other the evening of a grey autumn day, a road by the water-side and a couple of large oak trees." (Letter 066)

Seule (À Georges Lafenestre)

Les chaumes de velours, sous une poudre d'or,
Bordés d'un trait de feu, nagent dans l'ombre grise;
Par delà les toits noirs que sa lumière frise,
S'incline radieux l'astre de messidor.

Immense gerbe, il tombe épanchant son trésor:
Et le zénith bleu verse une lueur exquise
Sur la route où, parmi les senteurs de la brise,
Chante et bondit la ronde au tournoyant essor.

Dans la poussière ardente et les rayons de flammes,
Joyeusement, les mains aux mains, dansent les femmes.
Mais la plus belle rêve, assise un peu plus loin;

Elle est là, seule...et mord sa lèvre maladive,
Et telle qu'on verrait dans un champ de sainfoin,
Se crisper et languir la pâle sensitive.

      Courrières, 1873

Alone (To Georges Lafenestre)

It's harvest time, the stubble fields declare,
Fields bordered by sun's setting, lined with fire.
Black roofs are tinged with light as dusk approaches.
The star of harvest now is rising higher.
Huge sheaf, the evening star pours treasures out
And casts a bluish glow on land once sown
Where in late summer's fragrant cooling breeze,
Young women circle, singing on the road.

With joy they dance around the fire with hands
Held tight amid the dust and rays of flame.
But far off in the distance there is one,
Chewing her lip, yet lovely, like a dream,
Who sits alone, much like a single flower
In fields of hay—a delicate, pale bloom.

    Courrières, 1873

Seule/Alone

Seule, written in 1873, has a strong relationship to Breton's oil painting *The Feast of Saint John* (c. 1875) depicting young girls holding hands and dancing around a fire in the evening. (See: https://philamuseum.org/collection/object/102740) Introduced by the Catholic Church to honor the birth of John the Baptist, St John's Eve features bonfires of this type. Breton would have been well aware of this festival in his native Artois. It's origins are Greek, when a festival of fire would honor Apollo, the god of Music, and celebrate the summer solstice. In Breton's poem the round dancing is similar though the time of year appears to be closer to autumn. In the last line of his first stanza, Breton writes about *l'astre de messidor* (literally the star of Messidor or Messidor's star). Messidor was the tenth month in the French Republican calendar. Messidor is named after *messis*, a Latin word meaning harvest. Late summer's harvest may be the time period.

Georges Lafenestre (1837–1919) was a French art critic, art historian and poet. He was elected a member of the Académie des Beaux-Arts in 1892. His career was devoted to administering the fine arts as a curator at the Louvre and professor of the history of art at the École du Louvre, and a member of the Institut de France. Breton, too, was a member of the Académie and would have frequented the Louvre many times. Lafenestre also published the three volume *Parnasse contemporain* (*The Contemporary Parnassus*/The Contemporary Poetry Scene). His publisher was Alphonse Lemerre. Two of Breton's poems were included in the third volume. Lemerre was also editor and publisher of Breton's *Les Champs et la mer*.

There is no mention of Lafenestre in Van Gogh's letters but *Seule* might have appealed to him for a number of reasons. One of Van Gogh's paintings is titled *The Harvest* and he references other artists who have painted harvest landscapes including Israëls, Lhermitte, and Millet. In September 1882, Van Gogh wrote to Theo from The Hague, "Sometimes I can yearn for harvest time, that is, the time when I'll be so permeated by the study of nature that I myself will create something in a painting, yet analyzing things isn't a burden to me or something I dislike doing." (Letter 266)

Van Gogh included this poem in his letter to Van Rappard and it also appears in his second poetry album for Theo.

Le retour des champs (À François Millet)

C'est l'heure indécise où l'étoile
Pâle encor dans la pâle nuit,
Apparaît, scintille, se voile
Et fatigue l'œil qui la suit.

Entre les blés et la luzerne,
Bordé par les chardons poudreux,
Le chemin fauve se discerne
Encor dans les champs plantureux;

Le zénith couleur d'améthyste
Le caresse de son reflet
Inexprimable, que l'artiste
Ne peut qu'appeler violet.

Par la glèbe plane ou penchante,
Perdant, retrouvant ses sillons,
Il serpente dans l'herbe où chante
La note grêle des grillons.

Par les talus que le soir dore,
Il va, sous la clarté des cieux,
Où tinte la cloche sonore,
Au village silencieux.

Sous le crépuscule et le hâle,
Le paysan deux fois bruni,
Baignant son front dans le ciel pâle,
S'en revient, le travail fini.

Il porte la faux ou la bêche
A l'épaule; il va lentement,
Humectant sa poitrine sèche
De brume et d'odeur de froment.

Il va lentement, à son aise,
D'un pas tranquille en sa lourdeur;
Et l'occident, sourde fournaise,
Le bronze d'une sombre ardeur.

Sous le toit noir de sa chaumière,
Où fume un vague ruban bleu,
Brille un point de rouge lumière:
La soupe chante sur le feu.

Sa compagne est robuste et sûre
Et les enfants sont bien portants;
L'âge vient: que peut sa morsure
Près de l'enfance, gai printemps?

Tel il marche par habitude,
Tel il ira jusqu'au tombeau:
Content si, par son labeur rude,
Les blés sont lourds et l'orge beau.

Courrières, 1874

Return from the Fields (To François Millet)

It is the uncertain hour when the night
Grows pale and the pale star flickers in the sky,
Appears and flickers and then soon is veiled,
Wearying the tired follower's eye.

Bordered by the dusty, powdery thistles
Between the wheat, alfalfa and tall grass
Among the grain in fields so rich and fertile
One can perceive a fawn and tawny path.

Evening falls, caressing that tawny pathway.
Rays from on high the color of amethyst,
An inexpressible, unrepeatable color—
Radiant purple, calls out the artist.

The path crosses the smooth slope of the land.
It's lost then reappears in furrows and thickets.
Winding around it meanders through the grass
Where a shrill sound is heard, the song of crickets.

By embankments gilded with gold he goes.
It's now the evening, under the firmament.
In the village a church bell loudly tolls,
In the quiet village where all is usually silent.

The peasant walks along, his face twice burnished
Now by the twilight, then by the noonday sun.
The pale sky bathes his face, his day is finished.
Returning from the fields, his work is done.

Slowly he goes, weary he heads for home.
A scythe he bears, and on his shoulder it rests.
His chest, once dry, is wet now from the night air,
The scent of wheat heavy and rising in the mist.

Slowly he goes, slowly and at his ease.
He's calm, contented, yet heavy are his feet,
While the West like a fiery furnace burns,
Bronzing his skin with its deep and ardent heat.

Under the black roof of his cottage, where
Smoke billows, a blue ribbon rising higher,
Blazes a dot of red, a light, a glow
That warms the soup singing on the fire.

His spouse is robust, sturdy, firm and strong.
Old age approaches; why should he dread its sting?
His children are well and all are in good health,
Reminders of a bright and pleasant spring.

He treads through life by habit and by custom.
He will go to his death without a care,
Content because he knows by his hard labor
The wheat is heavy, and the barley fair.

Courrières, 1874

Le retour des champs/Return from the Fields

Jean-François Millet (1814–1875) was a French artist and one of the founders of the Barbizon school. Barbizon art focused on realism. *Le retour des champs* was written by Breton a year prior to Millet's death. Millet, like Breton, was well-known for his scenes of peasants working in the fields. Millet's art might well have been the inspiration for Breton's poem written in 1874.

Breton wrote that the first appearance of Millet's art "painted from nature, and not from the imagination" was in the 1853 Salon. Of Millet's art he wrote:

> With a plow standing in a rugged field where a few slender thistles are growing, two or three tones and an execution awkward and woolly, he can stir the depths of the soul and interpret the infinite....The wretched beings depicted by Millet touch us profoundly because he loved them profoundly, and because he has raised them to the higher regions inhabited by his genius, which has invested them with its own dignity. (*Autobiography*, pp. 224–226)

Millet was also one of Van Gogh's favorite artists and it is not surprising he chose this poem of Breton's to send to a fellow artist friend. In Van Gogh's letters Millet and Breton are often cited in the same sentence.

In his January, 1878 letter to Theo from Amsterdam, Van Gogh asks his brother to send him "The labourer" by Breton that Mauve, another artist, apparently had. The editors of this Van Gogh letter state that he was probably referring here to Breton's poem, *Le retour des champs*. Van Gogh also wrote to Theo about Millet's paintings of peasants with souls that animated the people he painted, echoing Breton's sentiments about Millet. (Letter 139)

Illusions (À Anatole France)

Qu'impétueusement un cœur blessé s'élance,
Lorsque l'hiver l'étreint sous son linceul épais,
Vers le premier asile où, jeune et dans la paix,
Il s'écoutait chanter au milieu du silence.

Avec quelle âpre ardeur, âme, tu te repais
Du toit natal, des prés et des fleurs bordant l'anse
De l'étang où l'oiseau sur les joncs se balance;
Et pourtant, ô Chimère, alors tu nous trompais!

Car dans ton beau mirage un avenir superbe,
Comme un été splendide ouvrait sa riche gerbe
Dont les épis flottants étaient de vrais soleils.

Tu mentais.—Mais qu'ils ont d'irrésistibles charmes
Ces fantômes qu'on voit dans les lointains vermeils
S'iriser à travers le grand prisme des larmes!

    Courrières, 1873

Illusions (To Anatole France)

Impetuously darts the wounded heart
Wrapped round with winter's shroud both thick and long,
To that first shelter where, when young, in peace,
It heard in the midst of silence its own song.

What ardent passion, soul, you once delighted in —
Your natal home where meadows and flowers weaved
Around the pond where the bird on the rushes swings,
And yet, O Chimera, you cheated us, you deceived!

Your fair mirage portended an excellent future,
A splendid summer, ushering in rich sheaves
Whose waving ears of grain were virtual suns.

You lied! But they have irresistible charms,
These ghosts we see in a distance, gilded by years,
Glimpsed through our pearlescent prism of tears.

    Courrières, 1873

Illusions/Illusions

In *Illusions* Breton wrote about *Ces fantômes qu'on voit dans les lointains vermeils* (these ghosts that we see in the ruddy distances), and reflected on years past that seemed to portend *un avenir superbe* (a great or excellent future).

Anatole France (1844–1924) was a French novelist, journalist and poet. Both Breton and France were brought up Catholic and attended private Catholic schools but it is unclear why Breton would have dedicated a poem to him. Breton often spoke of God's creative power and care for His creation. France, on the other hand, embraced atheism and socialism. He was, however, a member of the Académie Française. Breton was awarded the Montyon Prize for poetry by the Académie.

In December, 1875 Van Gogh wrote to Theo from Paris promising to send him Breton's complete book of poetry and noted the following: "Herewith what I promised. You'll like the book by Jules Breton. There's one poem of his that I found especially moving: 'Illusions.' Blessed are those whose hearts are thus attuned." (Letter 061)

He goes on in the same letter and writes: "All things work together for good to them that love God is a beautiful saying. It will be so for you, too; and the aftertaste of these difficult days will be good." At the time, Theo was under the care of a physician.

Breton's poem would have reminded both brothers of their childhood and their *du toit natal* (natal/childhood home).

Dans la plaine

A moi les champs, à moi les blés,
A moi les coteaux qui s'embrument,
Les faucheuses aux fronts hâlés,
Et les moissonneurs assemblés
Le soir, près des feux qu'ils allument!

A moi l'incendescant sillon
Où midi brûle le grillon,
A moi, tandis que l'oiseau chante,
Dans des flots verts, le vermillon
Du pavot à la fleur penchante !

A moi, loin de vos cœurs oisifs,
Pédants, à moi la plaine immense,
Prise de spasmes convulsifs,
Quant, la mordant, des feux lascifs
La font ondoyer en démence !

    1871

On the Plain

For me the fields—mine the fields of wheat.
For me the hillsides in the misty haze.
The women reapers, foreheads burned and tanned,
When evening falls draw round their fire's blaze.

For me the burning incandescent trail.
Vermilion poppies drop their heads and lean.
The cricket burns beneath the noonday sun.
For me the bird sings in the waves of green.

For me, far from your idle, slothful hearts,
Constricted, small — mine the immense plain.
And when the wanton acrid fires flare,
Fields undulate and sway as if insane.

1871

Dans la plaine / On the Plain

Dans la plaine was written by Breton in 1871 and may have been at least partial inspiration for one of his own oil paintings, *The Feast of Saint John* (1875) that depicts peasant women dancing around a fire holding hands. Originally a pagan festival, as noted in the commentary *Seule*, it became co-opted by Christians in the Middle Ages to celebrate the summer solstice (festival of fire). Breton would have been well aware of this festival in his native Artois. There is no dedication for this poem.

Breton, too, focuses on his own first love in his poem—not the city but the rural countryside and all it contained. Mine, he notes are the wheat fields, the hillsides, the immense plain and also the birds, insects and flowers. His focus, as in the majority of his paintings, is also on the peasantry, in this case women reapers, burned and tanned, in contrast, perhaps, to women of society carrying parasols to prevent the sun from blemishing their pale and delicate features.

Why might this poem have appealed to Van Gogh? Mary Ann Evans, known by her pen name George Eliot (1819–1880) was a leading writer of the Victorian era and a favorite author of Van Gogh. She wrote the following in her novel *Adam Bede*.

> Paint us an angel, if you can, with a floating violet robe, and a face paled by the celestial light...but do not impose on us any aesthetic rules which shall banish from the region of Art those old women scraping carrots with their work-worn hands...those rounded backs and stupid weather-beaten faces that have bent over the spade and done the rough work of the world... (Eliot, Book Second, XVII)

Van Gogh did paint a half figure of an angel after Rembrandt in 1889, but his main interest, like Eliot and Breton, lay with peasants like a family gathered around a table eating potatoes, rural farmers digging in the dirt, and women reaping in the fields. Eliot's further statement would also have appealed to both Van Gogh and Breton.

> In this world there are so many of these common coarse people, who have no picturesque sentimental wretchedness! It is so needful we should remember their existence, else we may happen to leave them quite out of our religion and philosophy and frame lofty theories which only fit a world of extremes. Therefore, let Art always remind us of them; therefore let us always have men ready to give the loving pains of a life to the faithful representing of commonplace things—men who see beauty in these commonplace things, and delight in showing how kindly the light of heaven falls on them. (Eliot, Book Second, XVII)

Crépuscule (À Charles Daubigny)

L'anémone et la renoncule
Ont fermé leurs fleurs de satin,
Voici le soir; le crépuscule
Idéalise le jardin.

Tout sommeille, même la brise,
Dans l'enivrement des parfums;
Et la couleur devient exquise
Dans la puissance des tons bruns.

Quand la nature se repose,
Lasse de jour et de splendeur,
Elle ouvre son âme et la rose
Dormant dans l'ombre a plus d'odeur.

Ainsi notre âme se réveille,
Lorsque nos sens sont assouvis,
Que des vains bruits frappant l'oreille
Nous ne sommes plus poursuivis.

Le Dieu devient discret et voile
Les inutiles ornements;
Tout s'agrandit; voici l'étoile.
Le ciel s'emplit de diamants.

La lumière pâle et diffuse
Baigne d'un charme tous les corps.
Et la silhouette s'accuse
Par un fil doré sur les bords.

Le mystère à chassé la prose;
Tout nage dans l'air savoureux
Et des lueurs d'apothéose
Émanent des fronts amoureux.

Et quelle fraîcheur ineffable
D'améthyste et de gris perlé,
Le zénith verse sur le sable,
A côté du gazon brûle!

Un rayon court dans l'ombre grise,
Plonge et meurt dans les profondeurs,
Faisant encore, lorsqu'il se brise,
Rejaillir de vives ardeurs.

Et les fleurs chuchotent discrètes,
Dans l'insaisissable flottant,
Dressant quelques rouges aigrettes,
Dernier effort du feu luttant.

Sur les buissons les éméraudes
Ont une sourde intensité;
Les fonds sont bruns; des vapeurs chaudes
Se traînent dans l'immensité.

Par delà les touffes d'érables.
Au ciel d'opale et d'or bruni,
Plein d'une tendresse adorable
Palpite et tremble l'infini.

Oh! ferme ta fleur, renoncule,
Amante du grand jour qui luit,
Pour ne pas voir au crépuscule,
Le Jour s'accoupler à la Nuit.

   Courrières, 1873

Twilight (To Charles Daubigny)

Anemone and buttercup
Have closed their satin flowers.
Evening is here and the garden
Becomes ideal in these twilight hours.

All slumbers, even the breeze
In perfumed air is drowned.
Evening colors become exquisite
In dusk's powerful shades of brown.

Weary from daylight's splendor,
Nature now takes her repose.
She opens her soul in the shadows
Where sleeps the most fragrant rose.

Thus our spirit, our soul awakens,
Though noise still strikes the ear.
Our senses are satisfied.
We've no longer cause to fear.

God discerns and throws a veil
Over things that don't beautify.
Evening waxes, her star emerges.
Soon diamonds fill the sky.

Bathing the world with charm,
Pale light diffuses, spreads.
Shadows appear and are tinged
All around with a golden thread.

All swims in delectable air.
Mystery banishes prose.
The gleam of apotheosis
From the faces of lovers flows.

And what ineffable freshness,
Pearl-gray and amethyst
Pours down from celestial spheres
On the sand, next to withered grass.

In the shadows the sun's short ray
Plunges and dies in the deep,
Scatters and yet once more
Casts back to the earth intense heat.

The flowers quietly whisper
In the air, elusive and floating,
Lift feathery plumes like red egrets
In the sunset's final closing.

On bushes, emerald hues
Have a veiled and muted intensity
Deepening into browns. Warm mist
Rises and trails through the density.

Beyond tufts of maple trees
Sky is tinged burnished-gold, flushed with opal.
Filled with delightful tenderness
Infinity palpitates and trembles.

O close your flower, buttercup
Lover of sun's great light
So you will not see the evening,
Day merging into the night.

Courrières, 1873

Crépuscule/Twilight

Breton begins this poem with a focus on the satin flowers of the anemone and buttercup. In his autobiography he writes about his childhood and the serious illness of his younger brother Louis that upset him greatly. Breton's uncle suggests they go for a walk to the marsh to help take his mind off his worries over his brother's illness. "My heart," wrote Breton, "was heavy" and then goes on to say; "We entered the wood where white and pale-violet anemones trembled as we passed." (*Autobiography*, p. 49)

He then writes about the delight experienced by the "reawakening of plant life" and how the "gardens especially rejoice the heart with inexpressible gladness" and notes that what most delights his eyes are "...the anemones that cluster around the shaft of the sun-dial." (p. 50)

Charles-François Daubigny (1817–1878) was a French printmaker and artist. A member of the Barbizon school, he was a precursor of impressionism. Realistic sunsets and evening scenes were popular subjects of his landscapes and this poem would have appealed to him with its focus on twilight. Daubigny was also known for his garden where he lived in Auvers. Auvers was where Breton was born.

Breton's poem would also have appealed to Van Gogh. In a July, 1883 letter to Theo, Vincent wrote the following:

> Rarely of late has the stillness, nature alone, so appealed to me. Sometimes it's precisely those spots where one no longer feels anything of what's known as the civilized world and has definitely left all that behind—sometimes it's precisely those spots that one needs to achieve calm. (Letter 369)

He goes on to state the following: "... but if I again feel the need to forget about the present and to think of the age of the beginning of the great revolution in art of which Millet, Daubigny, Breton, Troyon, Corot are the leaders, then I'll go back to that same spot."

Following Daubigny's death, Van Gogh visited his widow in Auvers and received permission to paint the Daubigny garden. He sent Theo a croquis (sketch) he had made of the garden in July, 1890. Van Gogh also painted two large canvases of Daubigny's garden and wrote Theo that he hoped he would see the oil paintings in the future. (Letters 898 & 902)

Le chant du soir

      Quand le nuage
          Surnage
Laissant flotter des lambeaux d'or;
      Qu'ouvrant sa gerbe
          Superbe,
Le soleil verse son trésor;

      Pauvres glaneuses,
          Faneuses,
Une riche gloire de feu
      Vibre et caresse
          La tresse
Ondoyante de vos cheveux.

      Le rayon rose
          Arrose
Vos vieux haillons traînant leurs fils,
      Glisse, flamboie
          Et noie
Dans la flamme vos beaux profils.

      Puis le mystère
          Austère
Tombe et se répand lentement;
      Au crépuscule
          Circule
La saine senteur du froment.

      Le massif d'ormes
          Énormes
Brunit ses rameaux emmêlés;
      Et d'un trait ferme,
          La ferme
S'accuse au sein vague des blés.

      Le feu fait trêve
          Le rêve
Se mêle aux effluves du soir;
      Le tout s'embrume
          Et fume
Ainsi qu'un immense encensoir

Le troupeau grêle
  Qui bêle
S'achemine vers le repos;
  Tandis que chante
   Touchante,
La douce flûte des crapauds.

  Puis monotone
   Résonne
Tout au loin la cloche à la tour;
  Et sa volée
   Ailée
S'élève et décroît alentour.

  La note tinte
   Éteinte,
Plus pure qu'aux bois lorsqu'encor,
  Dans l'ecarlate,
   Éclate
Au soir le son vibrant du cor.

  Aux hautes cimes
   Sublimes
Combien je préfère ce lieu,
  Cette humbe plaine
   Si pleine
De l'immense bonté de Dieu!

  Courrières, 1873

Song of the Evening

When the cloud drifts, it trails
Golden shreds like tattered
    Sails.
Magnificent and beyond measure,
Sun's beams pour out their
    Treasure.

Poor gleaners, reapers of hay,
Rich glory of sun's last
    Ray
Stirs, undulates your tresses,
Braids of your hair
    Caresses.

Tattered and ragged old clothes
Are bathed with rays of
    Rose.
Your beautiful profiles remain
Enveloped in day's last
    Flame.

Then slowly spreads the mystery.
Dusk transforms like
    Magistery
As the robust aroma of wheat
Now makes the day
    Complete.

The massive elm trees sough
Amid brown tangled
    Boughs.
Soft waves of wheat and corn
Reveal outlines of a
    Farm.

The evening fires wane.
Dreams mingle with smoke and
    Flame.
All around the fog grow denser
Like incense burned in a
    Censer.

The little flock of sheep
Moves toward rest, softly
    Bleats.
Toads now stir and sing.
Their gentle fluting songs
    Ring.

The church bell in the far tower
Resonates, tolling
    Hours.
It's volleys strike, repeat
On a monotonous
    Beat.

A note rings loud, then fades
In the forest and in the
    Glade,
Rings from a vibrating horn
Of a scarlet hunter,
    Adorned.

I prefer what is mine,
Not high peaks
    Sublime
But this plain and humble place
Filled with God's love and
    Grace.

        Courrières, 1873

Le chant du soir / Song of the Evening

Le chant du soir was written in 1873. There is no dedication. It seems to reflect many of Breton's pastimes and specific interests that were also subjects of his art. These included his love of nature and of beauty, of rural life and the peasantry, and also a belief in the grace and love of God. "What is the sky to me", he wrote, "if it does not give me the idea of infinity?" (*Autobiography*, p. 291)

"I have always had a passion for the Beautiful," Breton wrote in the closing pages of his autobiography. "I have always believed that the aim of art was to realize the expression of the Beautiful. I believe in the Beautiful — I feel it, I see it!" (p. 289) He also wrote about it.

James S. Taylor, in his book *Poetic Knowledge: The Recovery of Education*, wrote of the beautiful, the aweful (awefull), the spontaneous and the mysterious in relation to "the phenomenon of *poetic experience*" and tells us that poetic knowledge is the opposite of scientific knowledge in the empirical, quantifiable and didactic sense. (Taylor, pp. 5–6)

Breton would have agreed. So would Van Gogh. Frustrated by his desire to embark on a painting expedition due to lack of supplies, he wrote to Theo in 1883: "And so EVERYTHING IS PROSE, EVERYTHING IS CALCULATION in regard to the plan for a trip that after all has poetry as its goal." (Letter 391)

Van Gogh saw "infinite poetry" in the autumn or in a sunset and "so much soul and mysterious endeavor in nature." (Letter 559) In 1883, after his return from the Borinage region of Belgium, he wrote: "Poetry surrounds us everywhere..." (Letter 330) Of his 1888 painting *Willows at Sunset* he noted that "...and in all of nature, in trees for instance, I see expression and a soul, as it were. A row of pollard willows sometimes resembles a procession of orphan (almshouse) men." (Letter 292)

Breton's *Le chant du soir* would have appealed to Van Gogh as well. Van Gogh also loved nature and often reflected on this love in letters to friends and relatives. In one of his early letters to Theo written from London,

January 1874, Vincent speaks about the importance of nature to artists. "Always continue walking a lot and loving nature, for that's the real way to learn to understand art better and better. Painters understand nature and love it, and *teach us to see.*" (Letter 017) In an April letter from London he wrote: "It's absolutely beautiful here (even though it's in the city). There are lilacs and hawthorns and laburnums &c. blossoming in all the gardens, and the chestnut trees are magnificent. If one truly loves nature one finds beauty everywhere." (Letter 022)

One of Van Gogh's chief desires in life was to make others aware of the unquantifiable and poetic mystery of the universe that resides not only in seasons and sunsets but in people. For Van Gogh that might have been a potato digger or a weaver at his spinning wheel, "…serious subjects and so difficult, but so beautiful too that it's well worth the trouble of devoting one's life to depicting the poetry that's in them." (Letter 259) Breton would certainly have agreed as he communicated poetic mystery in both his canvasses and his poetry.

Les ruines

Les vieillards, quand près d'eux, semaine par semaine,
Le temps a dévasté, tour à tour, fleurs et fruits.
Les vieillards ont, ainsi que la cité romaine,
Au cœur un forum mort plein de temples détruits;

Silencieux désert où leur âme promène
Son long ennui stérile, où l'ortie et le buis,
Et l'herbe solitaire, en l'antique domaine,
Ont étouffé l'orgueil des fastes et des bruits;

Où des frontons muets la légende effacée
Sous la rouille des ans dérobe sa pensée.
Plus de chants, les oiseaux aiment les floraisons.

Plus de prisme charmeur irisant les bruines;
Mais de graves soleils, de vastes horizons,
Éclairant la beauté dernière des ruines.

The Ruins

When near them, week by week, old men are like ruins,
Like fruits and flowers decayed or withered by time.
Their hearts are like Roman cities with dead forums
Filled with temples destroyed and ravaged, left behind.

Their souls meander through a silent desert,
Barren, bored wasteland where nettles and box-weed sway
And the lonely grasses across their aged world
Have stilled their pompous noise once on display.

The rust of years has stolen the old men's thinking,
Erased their legends from silent impediments,
For singing birds love times of blooming.

No more charming, misty, iridescent prisms
But grave and sober suns with vast horizons
That illumine the final beauty of the ruins.

Les Ruines/The Ruins

Les ruines was published in *La Nouvelle Revue*, July 15, 1885. It is unclear why Breton would have written this poem; his usual focus in both his art and poetry was on the peasantry and French rural life. In his autobiography, when writing about his elders, he usually had high praise.

Van Gogh read the periodical in his father's house and would have seen the poem there. It is more understandable why he might have chosen this particular poem to send to his friend. He also copied this poem and sent it in a letter to his brother, Theo, in November, 1885. (Letter 543) The poem might have appealed to him because of its commentary on the negative aspects of aging. Van Gogh's relationship with his own father, Theodorus, was often contentious. Although they disagreed about many things, Vincent longed for his father's approval. His father's sudden death due to a massive stroke, in March, 1885 may have come prior to a full reconciliation.

In his letter to Theo, Van Gogh also mentioned hesitancy on the part of Catholic peasants in Nuenen that he wanted to use as models for his art; he noted their lack of courage to pose for him might have been related to the local priest who could have disapproved. The priest too, perhaps, was an older man or had the outlook of an older man hesitant to approve of artistic endeavors he thought might be morally questionable.

Les deux croix (À Robert-Fleury)

On voit, sur une route au pays de Pontcroix,
En plein ciel, toute neuve, une pompeuse croix
Où resplendit un Christ badigeonné de rose.
Deux ou trois pas plus loin, se tord, navrante chose,
Piteux et relégué sous les buissons d'un mur,
Laissant saillir de l'ombre un horrible fémur,
Penchant affreusement sa tête mutilée,
Au milieu de l'ortie à la ronce mêlée,
Oublié, l'ancien Christ informe et sans couleur.
Et l'éternel Souffrant, qui calme la douleur,
Rappelle, en cet état, les âpres agonies
De tant de nobles cœurs jetés aux gémonies;
Et le lépreux qui fuit le jour injurieux,
Le mendiant lui-même en détourne les yeux:
Et le poëte l'aime... et la foule qui passe
N'a de regards que pour celui qui dans l'espace
Étend ses bras en croix dans une gloire d'or.
Au crucifié même il faut un beau décor;
A celui-ci l'encens, les vœux et la prière;
L'autre, dans les cailloux, n'est qu'une vaine pierre.
Et cependant quel cœur ne serait pas touché!
Un trou s'ouvrait au mur, et le Christ l'a bouché!
Et l'égout du chemin, de sa fétide haleine,
Baigne ses pieds aimés qu'arrosa Madeleine.

Toi dont le crime fut de répandre l'amour,
Lorsque, pour t'en punir, Ponce et Caïphe, un jour,
Sur ta tête eurent mis la couronne d'épines,
O Christ! qu'un paysan de ses mains enfantines,
D'un barbare ciseau par l'amour ennobli,
Tailla dans ce bloc dur; croyais-tu que l'oubli
Oserait te jeter dans un trou de muraille,
Et qu'outrage dernier, l'insultante broussaille
Mêlerait sur ton front, qui saigne et qui bénit,
L'épine de la ronce à celle du granit?

Douarnenez, 1873

Two Crosses (To Robert-Fleury)

Along the road in the region of Pontcroix,
A pretentious cross looms large against the sky
With a gleaming rose-washed Christ, commanding awe.
But two or three steps farther on I spy,
Distorted, twisted, pitiful indeed,
Discarded under bushes by a wall,
A thigh bone in the shadows, and it leads
Me to another Christ among nettles and thorns,
An older Christ without color or form,
The Eternal Sufferer who calms all pain,
A Christ whose sad and sorry state recalls
His own and others' bitter agonies,
Those noble hearts cast into obloquy,
Forgotten, like this Christ who suffers shame.

The leper flees the light with head bent down.
The beggar's eyes will not gaze on this one.
The crowd just passes by with but a frown.
Saving their incense, vows and prayers, they shun
One loved of poets for one laved in gold,
Preferring a new setting, not the old.
And yet what heart would not be moved by this
Cold stone, this broken wall filled now with Christ?
Once watered with Magdalene's tears, ah, what a price!
These feet are now bathed with a sewer's fetid breath.

To punish you, Pilate and Caiaphas
placed on your head, one day, a thorn-wreathed crown.
What was your crime but to spread God's love around?
O Christ! With love a peasant, from a mass
Of stone, chiseled and carved you out, his rude
And clumsy child-like hands at work, yet now
You're lost in a dark cleft. O magnitude!
The final insult on your blessed brow,
A brow that blesses and a brow that bleeds,
Are prickly brambles that have become your crown,
And the rough-hewn granite wall among the weeds
That seeks to banish you into oblivion.

Douarnenez, 1873

Les deux croix/Two Crosses

We cannot tell from *Les deux crois* whether Breton was responding to something he actually saw traveling through Brittany or if it was a product of his imagination. Given the details it may have been the former or perhaps a bit of both. The Monastery Church of Notre-Dame de Roscudon, dating to the thirteenth century was in Pont-Croix; it is a large stone church featuring many stained glass windows and a 67-meter-high spire.

Tony Robert-Fleury (1837–1911) was an artist and painter of historical scenes. He was also a well-known art teacher. Breton's first paintings were historical paintings, similar in style and theme to Tony Robert-Fleury's. It is not clear, though, whether his dedication refers to Tony, the son, or to Joseph-Nicolas Robert-Fleury (1797–1890), the father, who was also a well-known artist. Robert-Fleury the elder was appointed professor and, in 1863, director of the École des Beaux-Art. Breton would have known about both father and son. The father's paintings were also historical in nature. There is no mention of either in Van Gogh's correspondence

Why would Breton's poem, *Les deux croix*, written in 1873, have appealed to Van Gogh? We have hints of this, I believe, in Van Gogh's original desire to become a pastor. Van Gogh was drawn to themes of suffering and salvation, even after he was dismissed from his position as an evangelist to miners in the Borinage by the Synodal Board of Evangelization, Union of Protestant Churches in Belgium (1879–1880) for his lack of public speaking skills. Though he had little use for the institutional church following his dismissal, both his art and letters indicate he was still drawn to Christ and Biblical themes. This was most evident at the end of his life when he was painting reproductions of art like Millet's *Angelus*, Delacroix's *Pietà* and *The Good Samaritan* and Rembrandt's *The Raising of Lazarus*.

Reflecting on Breton's two crosses and on his lowly peasant with childlike hands, chiseling and carving out Christ on His cross, could have led Van Gogh back to scripture, which played such a prominent role in his life prior to his role transition from pastor to painter. It could have also led him to contemplate the humble, suffering Christ of Isaiah 53 who had no form, no comeliness, nor beauty that we should desire him, much like the Christ of the rough-hewn carving, yet who drew people to him with meekness and lowliness of heart, supplying their souls with salvation and rest.

BOOK REFERENCES AND SELECT BIBLIOGRAPHY

For the original French poems and quotes by Jules Breton see:

Breton, Jules. *Les Champs et la mer*. Alphonse Lemerre, Éditeur. Paris, 1875. Nabu Primary Source edition. Nabu Public Domain Reprint

Breton, Jules. *Œuvres Poétiques de Jules Breton*, 1867–1887. Alphonse Lemerre, Éditeur. Paris, 1887. Wentworth Press. Imprint of Creative Media Partners. Public Domain Reprint, 2018.

Breton, Jules. *La Nouvelle Revue*, 7 (volume 35), July 15, 1885, p. 408.

Breton, Jules. *La Vie d'un artiste: Art et nature*. Alphonse Lemerre, Éditeur. 1890. Scholar Select. Reprint published by Wentworth Press. Imprint of Creative Media Partners

Breton, Jules. *The Life of an Artist: An Autobiography*. Translated by Mary J. Serrano. New York: D. Appleton and Company, 1890. Reprint published by Legare Street Press. Imprint of Creative Media Partners. Public domain in the United States

Pabst, Fieke, Editor. *Vincent van Gogh's poetry albums*. (Cahier Vincent 1). Rijksmuseum Vincent van Gogh in co-operation with the Vincent van Gogh Foundation. Uitgeverij Waanders, Zwolle, 1988.

For quotes from Vincent van Gogh's letters included in commentaries for each poem see:

Vincent van Gogh—The Letters. Leo Jansen, Hans Luijten, and Nienke Bakker, Editors. Van Gogh Museum & Huygens Institute, Amsterdam 2009: Version: October 2021: https://vangoghletters.org/ © Van Gogh Museum.

Breton's poems sent to Van Rappard from Van Gogh with non-metrical translations: See the Van Gogh letters website. Letter 435. https://vangoghletters.org/vg/letters/let435/letter.html

Additional References Consulted, Cited and Reviewed

Baer, William, Editor. *Thirteen on Form: Conversations with Poets*. Evansville: Measure Press, 2016.

Eliot, George. *Adam Bede* (1859). See: The Project Gutenberg eBook. 2023 https://www.gutenberg.org/cache/epub/507/pg507-images.html#link2HCH0017

Gayford, Martin. *The Yellow House: Van Gogh, Gauguin, and Nine Turbulent Weeks in Provence*. Boston: A Mariner Book. Houghton Mifflin Company, 2006.

Hulsker, Jan, Editor. *Van Gogh's "Diary": The Artist's Life in His Own Words and Art*. New York: William Morrow & Company, Inc., 1971.

Lacouture, Annette Bourrut. *Jules Breton: Painter of Peasant Life*. New Haven and London. Yale University Press in association with The National Gallery of Ireland, Dublin, 2002.

Mooney, Sharon Fish. *Bending Toward Heaven: Poems After the Art of Vincent van Gogh*. Eugene, OR: Wipf and Stock/Resource Publications, 2016.

Penot, Agnès, with Annette Bourrut Lacouture and Marie-Isabelle Pinet. "From Research to Publication: The Jules Breton Catalogue Raisonné, Forty Years in the Making," *Nineteenth-Century Art Worldwide*. Vol. 22, Issue 1 (Spring 2023) https://www.19thc-artworldwide.org/spring23/practicing-art-history-the-jules-breton-catalogue-raisonne

Plato. *Phaedrus*. Translated by Alexander Nehamas and Paul Woodruff. Hackett Publishing Company, Inc., UK ed., 1995.

Sturges, Hollister with contributions by Gabriel P. Weisberg, Annette Bourrut Lacouture, and Madeleine Fidell-Beaufort. *Jules Breton and the French Rural Tradition*. Joslyn Art Museum, Omaha, Nebraska in association with The Arts Publisher, Inc., New York, 1982.

Taylor, James S. *Poetic Knowledge: The Recovery of Education*. Albany: State University of New York Press, 1998.

Van der Veen, Wouter. *Van Gogh: A Literary Mind*. Literature in the correspondance of Vincent van Gogh. Van Gogh Studies 2. Waanders Publishers, Zwolle and the Van Gogh Museum, Amsterdam, 2009.

Weisberg, Gabriel P., Editor. *The European Realist Tradition*. Bloomington: Indiana University Press, 1982.

Additional Internet Resources:

Portrait of Jules Breton:
https://commons.wikimedia.org/wiki/File:Jules_Breton_001.jpg (Public Domain)

Jules Breton website: https//julesbreton.com

Bill Murray interview:
https://www.youtube.com/watch?v=8eOIcWB7jSA

TRANSLATOR'S POEM CREDITS

I wish to thank the following editors and journals where a number of my Breton translations with commentaries first appeared:

Transference. Published by the Department of World Languages and Literatures at Western Michigan University (*Automne/Autumn*). Fall 2019, Vol. 7. Molly Lynde-Recchia, Editor-in-Chief.

Delos: A Journal of Translation and World Literature. University of Florida Press. (*L'aube/Dawn; Illusions/Illusions; Le retour des champs/Return from the Fields*). Spring 2021, Vol. 36, No. 1. Judy Shoaf, Managing Editor.

Common Threads. Journal of the Ohio Poetry Association (*Les ruines/The Ruins; Soliel couchant/Sunset; Dans la plaine/On the Plain*). 2018, 2019, 2021. Steve Abbott, Editor.

Saint Austin Review (StAR). January/February 2023. (*Les deux croix/Two Crosses*). Joseph Pearce, Editor.

ACKNOWLEDGMENTS

Thank you to the following for a variety of reasons.

Alfred Nicol, poet and translator, for his helpful critiques of many of these poems and encouragement to pursue my French and translation studies.

Hans Luitjen, a senior researcher at the Van Gogh Museum, Amsterdam, co-editor of *Vincent van Gogh—The Letters*, and author of *Jo van Gogh-Bonger: The Woman Who Made Vincent Famous* (trans. by Lynne Richards)—for his assistance on my three visits to the Van Gogh Library. Van Gogh's letters and my discovery of his love for French poetry are directly responsible for my own translation journey.

Rhina P. Espaillat, poet and translator, for her advice and examples of metrical poetry translations.

Jennifer Grotz, poet, translator, and Director of the Bread Loaf Writers' Conferences, Middlebury College, Ripton, Vermont, who accepted my conference proposal of early Breton translations and to Geoffrey Brock, poet, translator, and workshop leader at Bread Loaf who gave me many helpful suggestions.

The Ohio Arts Council for an Individual Excellence Award for my poetry translations in 2018.

The formal-form poets and translators on the Able Muse/Eratosphere website who offered much helpful critique on a variety of my initial forays into French translation. (https://www.ablemuse.com/erato/)

The American Literary Translators Association (ALTA) for numerous opportunities to study translation and to translator Alexis Levitin who gave me much encouragement following my first bilingual reading at an ALTA. Conference. (https://www.literarytranslators.org)

Katherine M. Hedeen, ALTA workshop faculty, translator, Professor of Spanish at Kenyon College, and Managing Editor of *Action Books* who offered helpful critique of my translations.

Sherrel Rieger, Adult Program Specialist, Dover Public Library, Ohio, for many helpful poetry and translation reviews and speaking opportunities.

My husband, Scott, who has been my primary supporter and metrical mentor for many years of poetry writing and poetry readings.

ABOUT THE TRANSLATOR

Sharon Fish Mooney is the author of a book of sonnets: *Bending Toward Heaven: Poems After the Art of Vincent van Gogh* (Wipf and Stock/Resource Publications, 2016) and editor of *A Rustling and Waking Within* (OPA Press, 2017), an anthology of ekphrastic poetry by Ohio poets on art located in Ohio museums. She won the inaugural Frost Farm Prize for metrical poetry. She has lectured on Van Gogh, Breton, and ekphrastic poetry, and has read her poetry in university venues in the United States, Canada, France, and the Netherlands. Her poems have appeared in various journals including *Rattle, RUMINATE, First Things, Modern Age, The Lyric, The Lost Country, The Evansville Review, String Poet, The Ekphrastic Review,* and in various anthologies/chapbooks e.g. The Toledo Museum of Art and the Allen Memorial Art Museum, Oberlin, OH. Her poetry translations from the French have been published in the *Saint Austin Review* (StAR), the poetry journal *Common Threads*, and the translation journals *Delos* and *Transference.* Her PhD in nursing is from the University of Rochester. She teaches nursing research and education courses on-line for Regis University and Indiana Wesleyan University.

www.ingramcontent.com/pod-product-compliance
Lightning Source LLC
Chambersburg PA
CBHW061505040426
42450CB00008B/1495